*Presented to*

MEGAN KABEL

*by*

GRANDMA JUNE

*Date*

12/10/08

# The Picture
# BIBLE
for Little People

# The Picture BIBLE

## for Little People

## KENNETH N. TAYLOR

with illustrations by John Dillow

TYNDALE KIDS

Tyndale House Publishers, Inc.
Wheaton, Illinois

Visit Tyndale's exciting Web site at www.tyndale.com

Copyright © 2004 by Tyndale House Foundation. All rights reserved.

Cover and interior illustrations by John Dillow,
copyright © by Tyndale House Publishers, Inc. All rights reserved.

Edited by Erin Keeley Marshall

Cover design by Paetzold Associates, St. Charles, IL

Bible stories are adapted from My First Bible in Pictures by Kenneth N. Taylor,
copyright © 1989 by Tyndale House Publishers, Inc. All rights reserved. Text
copyright © 1989 owned by assignment by Tyndale House Foundation.
All rights reserved.

Printed in Singapore

ISBN 0-8423-8734-X
Children/Bible Story Books

Dear Children,

H ere is a book telling stories from God's holy book, the Bible. In it you will find exciting things that have happened to God's people. Sometimes God sends his mighty angels to protect them and keep them from danger. But you will also read about people who don't know very much about God, and so they do wrong things and get into a lot of trouble. Reading about them will make you want to tell them about Jesus who helps anyone who knows and loves him.

I hope this book will help you know and love Jesus even more than you do now, and that you will decide that all your life you will do whatever he wants you to do. And I hope that as soon as you can read well enough, you will read these stories directly from the Bible. Read the Bible all the way. Hint: start with the Gospel of Mark.

Many, many blessings upon you.

*Kenneth N. Taylor*

The artist has included a little white dove
in every picture in this book.
Can you find the dove in each illustration?
Sometimes they are very cleverly hidden.

God made the whole world. He made the land and the sky, the flowers and trees, and the animals. God even made the sun to give us daylight and the moon to shine at night. Everything God made was good.

*What are some things God made?*
**GENESIS 1:1-25**

God made the very first man and woman. Their names were Adam and Eve. God gave them the Garden of Eden as their home. The Garden had beautiful trees and plenty of food and water. Adam and Eve were very happy.

*Where did Adam and Eve live?*

**GENESIS 1–26-31; 2:7-8, 15, 18-23**

Adam and Eve did something God told them not to do. So God had to punish them. He sent them away from their home in the Garden of Eden. Then he sent angels to make sure Adam and Eve couldn't go back there.

*Why did Adam and Eve have to leave the garden?*
**GENESIS 2:9, 15-17; 3:1-24**

Cain and Abel were Adam and Eve's sons. Abel loved and obeyed God, but Cain was angry and killed Abel. This was wrong, and it made God sad. Cain had to leave that place and live somewhere else. From then on his life was very hard.

*What did Cain do wrong?*

**GENESIS 4:1-16**

13

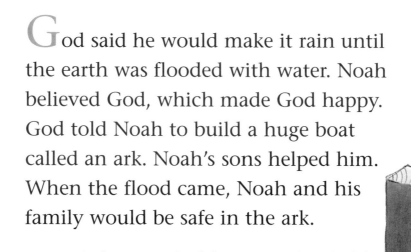

God said he would make it rain until the earth was flooded with water. Noah believed God, which made God happy. God told Noah to build a huge boat called an ark. Noah's sons helped him. When the flood came, Noah and his family would be safe in the ark.

*Why was God happy with Noah?*

**GENESIS 6:9-22**

15

When Noah finished building the ark, God told him to take two of each kind of animal and bird with him. After Noah and his family and the animals and birds were safe inside the boat, God shut the door.

*Who was on the ark?*
**GENESIS 7:1-16**

17

It rained for days and days. Water covered flowers and trees and even tall mountains. But Noah's ark floated on the water. God kept Noah and his family and the animals safe and dry in the boat. God takes care of you, too.

*Where was it safe from the rain?*
**GENESIS 7:17-24**

Abraham was God's friend. God told Abraham and his wife, Sarah, to move to another country. God promised to give Abraham the entire country so his children and his grandchildren and great-grandchildren could always live there. Abraham obeyed and believed God would take care of his family.

*Do you believe God keeps his promises?*
**GENESIS 12:1-9**

Abraham and Sarah were very sad because they didn't have any children. Many years earlier God had promised them a son. They waited a long time, but finally they had a baby! His name was Isaac. They were very happy because God answered their prayer and gave them a son.

*Why were Abraham and Sarah sad? What made them happy again?*

**GENESIS 15:1-6; 17:15-19; 21:1-7**

Isaac grew up and married Rebekah. They had twin sons named Jacob and Esau. After the boys grew up, Jacob had to leave home. He was very tired the first night. He dreamed about angels going up and coming down a stairway from heaven. Then God told Jacob, "I will protect you wherever you go."

*What did God say to Jacob?*

**GENESIS 28:1-5, 10-15**

Before Jacob left home, he had played a trick on his brother, Esau. Then Esau became angry. That's why Jacob left home and moved far away. After a long time, Jacob sent a message to Esau. The message said he hoped they could be friends again. Then they were happy to see each other.

*What can you do if someone is angry with you?*
**GENESIS 27:41; 33:1-11**

J acob had twelve sons. His favorite son was Joseph. He gave Joseph a beautiful coat. Joseph's brothers became angry because they didn't get special coats. So they were mean to Joseph.

*How do you think Joseph felt when his brothers were mean to him? Do you think he forgave them?*
**GENESIS 37:1-28**

A bad king wanted to kill baby Moses. To keep Moses safe, his mother put him in a basket in the river. God sent a princess to find the baby. The princess took care of Moses as he grew up.

*What did Moses' mother do to keep him safe?*
**EXODUS 2:1-10**

When Moses was grown up, he saw a bush on fire one day. But the bush didn't burn up! God talked to Moses from the bush. God said, "Help my people leave Egypt." Moses was afraid, but God promised to help him.

*What did God promise when Moses was afraid?*

**EXODUS 3:1-15**

God's people were treated very badly by Pharaoh, the king of Egypt. Pharaoh's soldiers whipped the people to make them work hard. God sent Moses to help his people. He told Moses to lead them out of Egypt and away from Pharaoh.

*What can you do to help someone?*

**EXODUS 5:6-14; 6:1-13**

Moses told Pharaoh to let God's people leave Egypt. When Pharaoh said no, God sent lots of problems to bother Pharaoh and the other Egyptian people. Frogs and flies filled the land, and hail ruined the farmers' crops. But Pharaoh still said no. Finally God said the oldest boy in each Egyptian family would die.

*What did Pharaoh say when Moses told him to let the people go?*
**EXODUS 7:14–11:5**

God was punishing the Egyptians. But he didn't want to hurt his own people. Moses told God's people to put lamb's blood on their doors. If they obeyed, God would keep them safe. The night this happened is called the Passover because the angel of death passed over the houses with the blood on the door. Finally Pharaoh let God's people go. They left that very night!

*Does God keep you safe?*
**EXODUS 12:1-13, 28-42**

Moses led God's people to the Red Sea. They needed God's help to cross it. When Moses held up his stick, God made a dry path through the water. All the people made it safely across to the other side.

*How did God help his people cross the Sea?*

**EXODUS 14:5-31**

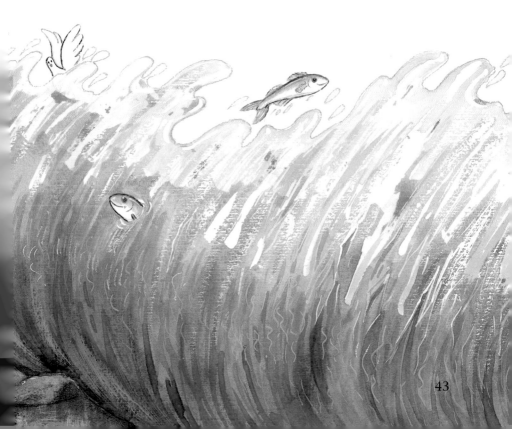

43

God's people were hungry as they traveled away from Egypt. So God took care of them by sending food each day. The food was bread called manna. Every morning the people would pick up enough manna for that day.

*What did God do to give his people food?*

**EXODUS 16:1-31**

God's people were very thirsty, but they couldn't find any water. God took care of his people again. He told Moses to hit a rock with his stick. When Moses did that, water flowed out of the rock. Then everyone had plenty to drink. Ah-h!

*How did God give people water to drink?*

**EXODUS 17:1-6**

46

God told Moses ten very important rules that he wanted his people to obey. God wrote those ten rules on pieces of stone. Those rules are called the Ten Commandments. One rule says to love God more than anyone or anything else. Another rule says to obey your mom and dad.

*What is one of God's rules?*

**EXODUS 20:1-17**

While Moses was getting the stones with God's rules written on them, the people created an idol that looked like a young cow. They worshiped the idol instead of worshiping God. That made God angry and sad. The people broke the rule that said to worship only God.

*What did the people do that made God angry and sad?*

**EXODUS 31:18–32:20**

$A$ church is called God's house. God's first house was called the Tabernacle. It was a beautiful tent. Moses' brother, Aaron, helped the people to worship God there. They thanked God and prayed to him at the Tabernacle.

*What do you do at church?*

**EXODUS 35:1-3, 20-35; 36:2-7; 40:30-33**

Moses kept leading the people on their long trip through the wilderness. God helped them. He put a cloud in the sky for them to follow during the day. Each night the cloud turned to fire. Moses and the people went wherever God moved the cloud.

*How did God show the people where to go?*

**EXODUS 40:34-38**

God wanted his people to learn about the land he promised to give them, so Moses sent twelve men there. When they came back, Joshua and Caleb were the only ones who said how wonderful it was. Joshua and Caleb knew God would take care of them. The other ten men didn't think God would help them.

*What did Joshua and Caleb tell the people?*

**NUMBERS 13:1-3, 25-33; 14:1-9**

Snakes were biting God's people and killing them. Once again God took care of them. He told Moses to make a metal snake and put it on top of a pole. When the people who were bitten looked at the snake on the pole, God made them well again.

*How did God make the people well again?*

**NUMBERS 21:4-9**

58

Balaam was going somewhere God didn't want him to go. So God sent an angel to stop him. When Balaam's donkey saw the angel, it stopped. Balaam hit the animal to make it go again. Then the donkey talked! "What have I done?" it asked. Finally Balaam saw the angel and listened to his message.

*What did the donkey see before Balaam saw it?*

**NUMBERS 22:9-38**

After Moses died, Joshua became the new leader of God's people. God told him to destroy Jericho. Joshua and all the people marched around the city's walls, blowing horns and shouting. Suddenly the huge walls tumbled down! Then God's people went inside.

*How did Joshua lead his people into Jericho?*

**JOSHUA 6:1-24**

$G$ideon wanted to take ten thousand soldiers with him to fight their enemies. But God wanted his people to know that he was powerful. He told Gideon to choose only the three hundred men who drank water from their hands. God said he would help them win the battle. And he did!

*Which soldiers did God let Gideon choose?*

**JUDGES 7:1-22**

Samson was really strong! He could break through ropes that tied him up. One time he killed a fierce lion with his bare hands. He was even strong enough to knock down a palace to punish God's enemies. God made Samson strong so he could help God's people.

*Why did God make Samson strong?*
**JUDGES 14:5-6; 15:11-14; 16:19-30**

Job loved God and always tried to do what God said. But Job had a lot of problems. He got very sick and lost a lot of money and all his children. Even though Job was very sad, he still loved God. Then God healed Job and made him happy again.

*Who made Job happy again?*

**JOB 1:6-22; 2:7-10; 42:1-17**

Naomi was sad. Her husband and her two sons had died. She was going back to the place she had come from. Ruth stayed with Naomi and was kind to her. God was happy that Ruth was a helper. God took care of both women because he is a helper too.

*Who can you help?*
**RUTH 1:1–2:18**

Samuel lived at the tabernacle and helped Eli the priest. One night Samuel woke up when he heard a voice. "Samuel! Samuel!" the voice said. At first he thought Eli was calling him. But then he knew it was God's voice. Samuel answered and said, "Here I am. What do you want me to do?"

*What did Samuel say to God?*
**1 SAMUEL 3:1-10**

God's people wanted a king. God knew that was not a good idea, but he gave the people what they wanted. He chose Saul to be the king. Saul was tall and strong and handsome. But he did many wrong things as king.

*Did God think it was a good idea for his people to have a king?*

**1 SAMUEL 8:4-9; 9:2; 10:1; 13:11-14**

74

When David was young, his job was to take care of his father's sheep. He kept them safe from wild animals. David also wrote beautiful songs about God's love. Many of his songs are in the Bible. David was God's friend.

*What did David write songs about?*

**1 SAMUEL 16:1-13; PSALM 23**

One day while David was watching the sheep, a hungry lion came nearby. The lion tried to eat the sheep. But God gave David strength and helped him to be brave. God helped David kill the lion and protect the sheep.

*Who helped David be strong and brave?*

**1 SAMUEL 17:32-37**

Goliath was a giant! He was also one of God's enemies. He wanted to fight God's people. God's soldiers were scared of Goliath. But David knew that God would help him fight the mean giant. David used his slingshot to throw a stone at Goliath. The stone hit Goliath's head and killed him.

*Did God help David?*
**1 SAMUEL 17:38-49**

One of David's friends was Jonathan, King Saul's son. King Saul didn't like David. When the king tried to kill David, Jonathan helped David hide. Jonathan also gave David his robe and sword.

*Are friends kind to each other?*

**1 SAMUEL 18:1-4; 20:16-25, 33-42**

One night when David was hiding from King Saul, he saw the king sleeping. David could have hurt King Saul, but he knew God didn't want him to do that. David obeyed God and left the king alone.

*Did David obey God?*

**1 SAMUEL 26:5-25**

God did not want Saul to be the king anymore. God told old Samuel that David would be the next king. So Samuel sent for David. God had Samuel pour olive oil on David's head to get him ready to be king. God would help David do a good job.

*What did God tell Samuel?*
**1 SAMUEL 16:1-13**

When King Saul died in battle, David became the new king. He wanted the rules that God gave to Moses to be near him. So David brought the box with the rules inside to the city of Jerusalem. God's people were excited. They celebrated and danced with joy.

*Why did the people celebrate?*
**2 SAMUEL 6:1-15**

King David saw Bathsheba taking a bath. He thought she was beautiful, and he wanted to marry her. But Bathsheba was already married. So David did something awful. He made sure her husband was killed in battle. God was angry. But when David was sorry for what he had done, God forgave him.

*What did God do when David was sorry?*

**2 SAMUEL 11:2-27; 12:13; PSALM 51:1-17**

Absalom was King David's son. He
wanted to be king instead of his father.
So David's soldiers were chasing him.
They knew he had not obeyed his father.
Absalom's hair got caught in some tree
branches, and his donkey kept going
without him. Then King David's army
found Absalom hanging by his hair from
the tree.

*Why was Absalom
running from the soldiers?*
**2 SAMUEL 18:1-9**

David and Bathsheba had a son named Solomon. God's helper put oil on Solomon's head to show that he would be the next king. When Solomon became the new king, he asked God to make him wise. God was happy to give the new king wisdom.

*What did God give Solomon?*

**1 KINGS 1:28-40; 2:10-12; 3:3-14**

Sometimes wise King Solomon solved problems for people. One day two women were fighting over a baby. They both wanted to be the baby's mother. God helped King Solomon know which woman was the real mother. He gave the baby to her.

*Who made King Solomon wise enough to know who was the baby's mother?*

**1 KINGS 3:16-28**

# King Solomon built a beautiful Temple
where people worshiped God. He prayed to
God there and praised him for being so
loving and kind. God told Solomon to
obey him. Then God would keep all the
promises he had made to Solomon's father,
David, when he was king.

*What did King Solomon do*
*at the Temple?*
**1 KINGS 6:37-38; 8:22-30; 9:1-5**

When Solomon obeyed God he was a good king. But sometimes Solomon did wrong things. He prayed to animals made of gold. But God is the only one people should pray to. God was angry and told Solomon he would take away his kingdom.

*Why was God angry with Solomon?*
**1 KINGS 11:9-13**

Elijah was a prophet. He was one of God's helpers. Elijah told the king that it would not rain for a long time because of all the wrong things the king did. God told Elijah to hide from the angry king. When Elijah was hungry, God had birds bring food to him.

*God took care of Elijah.*
*Will God take care of you?*
**1 KINGS 17:1-6**

Elijah wanted to show everyone that God is powerful. So he told people to pour water on some wood and stones. Then he asked God to send fire from heaven. Even though water puts out fires, that fire God sent burned up the water!

*What did Elijah want to show everyone?*

**1 KINGS 18:30-39**

It was time for Elijah to go to heaven.
So God sent horses and a wagon called a
chariot, all made of fire. Elijah rode away
in the chariot. Elijah is in heaven now.
God chose Elisha to be his new helper.
Elisha watched the chariot carry Elijah
up to God.

*Where did Elijah go?*
**2 KINGS 2:1-12**

God's new helper, Elisha, met a woman who didn't have any money. All she had was a jar of oil. Elisha told her to fill a lot of jars with the oil. She poured and poured, but God made her jar stay full! Then Elisha told her to sell the oil and earn money to live.

*What did God do for the woman?*
**2 KINGS 4:1-7**

Elisha had friends in one of the towns he visited. They let him stay at their house. One day their son died.
It was very sad. But God did something wonderful. When Elisha prayed, God made the boy alive again!

*What was the wonderful thing God did for Elisha's friends?*

**2 KINGS 4:8-37**

Naaman was in charge of the king's soldiers. But he got very sick with sores on his body. A little girl told Naaman that Elisha could make him well. Elisha told Naaman to wash seven times in the Jordan River. At first that made Naaman angry. But when he obeyed, God healed his sores.

*Who healed Naaman?*
2 KINGS 5:1-14

Some men were using axes to chop down trees. One man's ax fell into the river, and it sank to the bottom. But Elisha, God's helper, knew God can do anything. So Elisha threw a stick into the water. Then God made the ax float to the top.

*Is God powerful enough to do anything?*

**2 KINGS 6:1-7**

God won a great battle for his people. They were so thankful to him for his help. The people celebrated with music and marched into the city of Jerusalem. They went to the Temple to thank God and praise him for what he had done for them.

*Why did the people thank God?*
**2 CHRONICLES 20:20-30**

When King Joash was a baby prince, his wicked grandmother wanted to kill him! But his kind aunt hid Joash in the Temple until he was seven. When Joash became king, the soldiers took his grandmother away so he would be safe.

*Where did Joash's aunt hide him?*

**2 KINGS 11:1-16**

King Joash was a good king. He wanted God's temple to be repaired. The people gave money to make the Temple beautiful again. Then everyone could go there to thank God for being so kind and loving to his people.

*What can you thank God for?*
**2 KINGS 12:1-16**

God told Jonah to go to Nineveh. But Jonah didn't want to obey. Instead he sailed away on a boat. Then God sent a storm on the sea. Jonah fell into the water, where a big fish swallowed him. After three days the fish spit Jonah onto the sand. Jonah knew it was time to obey!

*What did Jonah do wrong?*

**JONAH 1:1–3:3**

King Ahaz was very bad. He didn't love God, and he wouldn't let people pray to God. He even told his workers to nail the Temple doors shut. God punished King Ahaz for the terrible things he did.

*Was King Ahaz a good king?*

**2 CHRONICLES 28:1-5, 16, 21-25**

King Hezekiah was a good king who loved God. Many other kings worshiped fake gods called idols. And they taught God's people to pray to the idols. They thought the idols could help them. But Hezekiah knew God was the only one to worship. So King Hezekiah's men smashed the idols.

*Is God the only one to worship?*

**2 KINGS 28:1-5, 16, 21-25**

King Josiah wanted to obey God. But God's rules had been lost for a long time. Finally someone found them. When Josiah learned the rules, he was sorry that he had not obeyed all of them. When he asked God to forgive him, God did!

*Is it important to know God's rules and obey them?*

**2 KINGS 22:1-20**

Jeremiah was one of God's brave helpers. He told the people messages from God. Some people didn't like what he said. So they put him in a deep, dark hole. But the king let Jeremiah out. After that, Jeremiah kept telling people what God wanted them to do.

*Will you be brave and tell people about God?*

**JEREMIAH 38:1-18**

God was not happy with his people. They prayed to pictures or carvings of animals and birds instead of God, and that made God sad and angry. So he let their enemies burn the city of Jerusalem. But Jeremiah loved God. Because Jeremiah obeyed, God promised to keep him safe.

*What is happening to the beautiful city?*

**JEREMIAH 39:4-5, 8-18**

Daniel and his three friends lived far
away from their home. The king burned
Jerusalem, where they used to live.
Daniel and his friends loved and obeyed
God. So God helped them give good
advice to the king. Then the king liked
them.

*How did God help Daniel and his
friends?*
**DANIEL 1:1-21**

Shadrach, Meshach, and Abednego were Daniel's friends. They had a problem. The king made a rule that everyone must pray to a statue that looked like him. But Shadrach, Meshach, and Abednego prayed only to God. That made the king angry! But Daniel's three friends still would not obey the bad rule.

*Who did Shadrach, Meshach, and Abednego pray to?*
**DANIEL 3:1-18**

The king threw Shadrach, Meshach, and Abednego into a very hot fire because they wouldn't pray to his statue. But when he checked on them, the king saw an extra person in the fire! God had sent an angel to take care of the three friends! He kept them safe!

*Did the fire hurt Shadrach, Meshach, and Abednego?*

**DANIEL 3:19-30**

$A$ new king gave a big party. While everyone was celebrating, they saw a hand that was writing on the wall. The king was afraid. So he asked Daniel what the writing meant. God helped Daniel understand. Daniel told the king that the words said he couldn't be king anymore.

*Why was the king afraid?*
**DANIEL 5:1-6, 10-30**

The king wanted everyone to pray to him, but Daniel loved God and prayed only to him. The king's men punished Daniel for praying to God. They threw him into a den filled with hungry lions. But was Daniel hurt? No! God sent an angel to protect him.

*Did God let the lions hurt Daniel?*
**DANIEL 6:1-23**

Queen Esther was kind and beautiful. She loved God and was very brave even when she felt scared. When God's people were in danger, Esther asked the king to help them. The king made a new law to save the people.

*Was Esther brave even when she was scared?*

**ESTHER 5:1-8; 7:1-4; 8:3-16**

144

The old Temple had been ruined. So God's people built a beautiful new Temple. It was their new church where they could praise him and thank him. The people wanted God to be happy with the Temple, so they worked very hard on it to please him.

*Is God glad when we thank him?*
EZRA 6:7-10, 14-16

The angel Gabriel had good news for Mary from God. At first Mary was afraid of Gabriel. But Gabriel told her, "Don't be frightened. You will be the mother of God's Son, Jesus!" That made Mary very excited! She told Gabriel she would do whatever God asked.

*Why was Mary excited?*
LUKE 1:26-38

Zechariah and Elizabeth had a baby
boy when they were very old. An angel
had told Zechariah he should name the
baby John. God had a special job for
John to do. John was to tell people that
Jesus was coming.

*What was John's special job?*
**LUKE 1:5-20, 57-79**

Mary and Joseph were in Bethlehem when Mary was ready to have her baby. But they didn't have a place to stay because the inn was full. The only place to stay was a barn where animals lived. Jesus, God's Son, was born that night.

*Where were Mary and Joseph staying when Jesus was born?*
**LUKE 2:4-7**

$S$ome shepherds were taking care of their sheep near Bethlehem, where Jesus was born. Suddenly they saw an angel. He told them baby Jesus had been born that night. Then other angels filled the sky. They praised God for sending Jesus to save us from our sins.

*Why did the angels praise God?*

**LUKE 2:8-14**

The shepherds were very excited! Right away they hurried to Bethlehem to find the baby. They found him in a barn, just like the angel said. The shepherds knew he was God's Son. They told everyone the good news that Jesus was born.

*How did the shepherds know where Jesus was?*

**LUKE 2:15-20**

Simeon was a very old man when Jesus was born. He had waited a long time to see God's Son. Simeon was so happy when he saw Mary and Joseph with Jesus. He thanked God for sending his Son to be our Savior.

*What did Simeon thank God for?*

**LUKE 2:25-32**

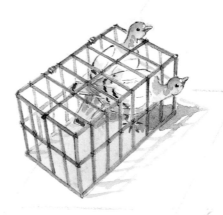

$S$ome wise men from faraway places heard that Jesus had been born. They followed a special star that led them to Jesus. The wise men brought presents for Jesus because they knew he was a very important king.

*What did the wise men follow to find Jesus?*

**MATTHEW 2:1-12**

Many people loved Jesus, but some people did not. A wicked king wanted to kill him. God sent an angel, who told Joseph to take Mary and Jesus to Egypt. It was not safe for them to stay in Bethlehem anymore. Joseph obeyed. God helped Joseph and Mary take good care of his Son.

*What did God's angel tell Joseph?*
**MATTHEW 2:13-15**

After a while Jesus and his family left Egypt and went back to their home in Nazareth, where Joseph was a carpenter. As Jesus grew bigger, he learned many things from Mary and Joseph. Everyone loved him. God did too!

*Where did Jesus grow up?*
**MATTHEW 2:19-23; 13:55; LUKE 2:52**

When Jesus was twelve years old, he went to the Temple with his family. He talked to the teachers and asked them a lot of questions. They were amazed that Jesus knew so much about God. They didn't know he was God's Son!

*Did the teachers know Jesus was God's Son?*

**LUKE 2:41-51**

Jesus and John the Baptist were cousins. When Jesus was older, John baptized him in the Jordan River. The Holy Spirit came down from heaven as a dove. God's voice from heaven said, "Jesus is my dear Son. I love him and am pleased with him."

*What did God say about Jesus?*
**LUKE 3:21-22**

Nicodemus visited Jesus one night. He wanted to know how to get to heaven. Jesus told him that God loves everyone so much that he sent Jesus to die for our sins. Anyone who believes in Jesus, God's Son, will get to live in heaven someday!

*Who will get to live in heaven?*
**JOHN 3:1-17**

Twelve of Jesus' friends were called disciples. They went everywhere with him. He taught them about God and heaven. The disciples saw Jesus do many miracles like healing sick people and helping blind people see again. Jesus knew the disciples would tell everyone about him someday.

*Who went everywhere with Jesus?*
**MARK 3:7-19**

One day Jesus was resting by a well. A woman came to get water from the well. Jesus was thirsty, so he asked her for some water. Then he told her he could give her joy that would never go away. The woman believed Jesus and told her friends the happy news. They believed in Jesus too.

*What good news did Jesus tell the woman?*

**JOHN 4:1-42**

Some fisherman had been fishing all night, but they didn't catch anything. They were very tired. But then Jesus got into their boat and told them what to do. When they listened to Jesus, they caught more fish than their nets could carry! They decided to follow Jesus after that.

*What happened when the fishermen listened to Jesus?*
**LUKE 5:1-11**

177

Jesus talked about God with everyone he met. Sometimes he taught big groups of people. He told them that God loves kindness. He doesn't want people to be nasty or argue. Jesus wants us to be kind to others, just like we want them to be kind to us.

*How does Jesus want us to treat others?*

**MATTHEW 5:1-26; 7:12**

A man had a little daughter who was very sick. He asked Jesus to heal her, but she had already died. Jesus went to her house anyway. When he spoke to her and said, "Get up, my child!" the little girl was alive and healthy again!

*What did Jesus say to the girl?*
**LUKE 8:40-44, 48-56**

Jesus met a man who was blind. The man couldn't see anything. Some of his friends asked Jesus to help him see again. When Jesus put his hands on the man's eyes, he could see everything! His eyes worked perfectly, and he could see trees and animals and flowers and Jesus.

*What did Jesus do for the blind man?*
**MARK 8:22-26**

Jesus and his disciples were in a boat during a big storm. The disciples were scared of the huge waves. But Jesus was sleeping. They woke Jesus up. "We are going to drown!" they screamed. So Jesus told the storm to stop. Then everything was peaceful and quiet.

*What did Jesus do when the disciples woke him up?*
**LUKE 8:22-25**

The disciples were in a boat during another storm. They were scared of the waves again. But they were even more scared when they saw someone walking toward them on top of the water! It was Jesus! He made them feel better when he said, "I am here! Don't be afraid." They were safe with Jesus.

*Does Jesus keep his disciples safe?*

**MATTHEW 14:22-33**

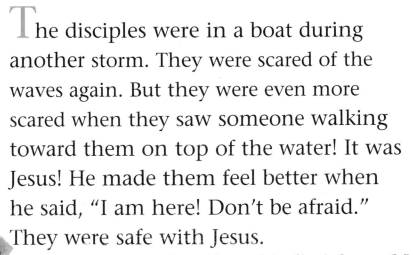

People followed Jesus wherever he went. One time a big crowd was hungry, but they didn't have any food. Then a little boy gave his lunch to Jesus. It was only two fish and five pieces of bread. But Jesus used the little lunch to make enough to feed everyone. And there were many baskets full of leftovers!

*What did Jesus do to feed the people?*
**JOHN 6:1-13**

A woman whose husband had died was very poor. She had only two pennies. Even though her life was hard, she was thankful for everything God gave her. She gave her two pennies to the church. God was happier with her than with the rich people who gave only a small part of their money.

*Do you give money to Jesus at Sunday School?*

**LUKE 21:1-4**

Children are special to Jesus! Some mothers brought their children to see Jesus. But his disciples didn't think they were important. The disciples told them to go away. But Jesus called the children and hugged them. He loved them and said they could believe in him just like grown-ups.

*Are you glad that Jesus loves you?*
**LUKE 18:15-17**

A man was lying on the side of the road. Robbers had stolen his money and hurt him badly. Some people passed by but did not help him. Then one of the man's enemies saw him. He put bandages on the man's cuts and bruises and took care of him. That kind person is known as the Good Samaritan.

*Can you be a Good Samaritan by helping people?*
**LUKE 10:25-37**

One day Jesus was visiting his friends Mary and Martha. Martha was angry with her sister, Mary, because Mary was listening to Jesus. Martha thought Mary should help her cook dinner instead. But Jesus was happy that Mary knew it was better to spend time with him.

*Why was Jesus happy with Mary?*
**LUKE 10:38-42**

A good shepherd takes care of his sheep. No matter where they go, he looks for them if they are lost. He helps the lambs if they get hurt. Jesus is our Good Shepherd. We are his sheep. Jesus knows everything about us and loves us very much.

*Does Jesus know everything about you?*

**JOHN 10:1-16**

Lazarus was Mary and Martha's brother. He was also one of Jesus' friends. But Lazarus died. His sisters and Jesus were very sad. But Jesus can do anything. So he went to the grave and called, "Lazarus! Come out!" Then Lazarus was alive again and walked out of the grave!

*What did Lazarus do when Jesus called to him?*

**JOHN 11:1-44**

Ten men who were very sick asked Jesus to heal them. Jesus told them to show the pastor that they were all better. As the men walked away, their sores disappeared and they were healthy again. But only one man thanked Jesus. Jesus wished the others had remembered to be thankful.

*Do you remember to thank Jesus for the good things he does for you?*

**LUKE 17:11-19**

A rich man wondered how he could get to heaven. Jesus knew the man was greedy. So Jesus told him to give his money to the poor people and follow God. The rich man walked away very sad. He loved his money more than he loved doing what pleased God.

*Is it important to love God more than anything else?*

**LUKE 18:18-27**

A man had two sons whom he loved. His younger son asked him for a lot of money. Then the son moved far away and wasted the money doing bad things. Finally he went home and told his father he had been wrong. His father hugged him and was so happy to see him!

*Was the father happy his son finally came home?*

**LUKE 15:11-24**

Zacchaeus took a lot of money from people. No one liked him. But Zacchaeus wanted to see Jesus. So he climbed a tree to see over the crowd. Jesus saw him in the tree and said, "I'm coming to your house." After he met Jesus, Zacchaeus gave back to the people more money than he had taken.

*What did Zacchaeus do after he met Jesus?*
**LUKE 19:1-10**

Many people gathered around Jesus as he rode into Jerusalem on a donkey. They waved palm branches and sang praises to him. They wanted Jesus to be their new king. They thanked God for sending him.

*What did the people do when Jesus rode into Jerusalem?*

**LUKE 19:28-38**

Jesus wanted his disciples to know that it's important to help other people. He showed them his kindness by washing their feet. They knew that meant he cared about them. Jesus likes it when we show people we love them.

*What kind things can you do for your family?*
**JOHN 13:1-17**

Jesus knew he was going to die soon. One night he was eating supper with his disciples for the last time on earth. He told them that the soldiers would come to take him away soon. Then he would be killed. He held a cup of red wine he was going to drink to show that he would give his red blood to wash away our sins.

*Why did Jesus die?*
**LUKE 22:14-20**

Jesus was sad that the soldiers would take him away soon. He prayed and told God how he was feeling. He asked God to help him. God sent an angel to help Jesus be strong. Jesus obeyed even when it was very hard for him.

*How did God help Jesus?*

**LUKE 22:39-46**

One of the disciples was not a good man. Judas was a disciple, but he didn't really love Jesus. Jesus' enemies paid Judas money to tell them where Jesus was. When the soldiers came, Judas led them to Jesus and kissed him to show the soldiers which man was Jesus. The other disciples were not very brave. They ran away.

*Did Jesus' friends help him when the soldiers came?*

**MATTHEW 26:47-56**

Peter was one of Jesus' friends who was not brave when the soldiers came. He was afraid the soldiers would hurt him too. Peter lied. He told three people, "I don't know Jesus!" Peter was sorry after that. He became brave and told many people about Jesus!

*Is it wrong to tell a lie?*
**LUKE 22:54-62; ACTS 2:14-24**

The soldiers brought Jesus to Pilate. Pilate was a judge. He knew Jesus hadn't done anything wrong. But he didn't want to make the people angry. The crowd kept shouting that they wanted Jesus to die. So Pilate told the soldiers they could kill Jesus.

*Did Pilate do the right thing?*
**LUKE 23:1-25**

The soldiers nailed Jesus to a cross of wood. It hurt Jesus a lot. But Jesus loves us. So he let God punish him instead of punishing us for the wrong things we do. Jesus never did anything wrong. But he died for us anyway.

*Why did Jesus die?*
**MARK 15:24; LUKE 23:34-46**

After Jesus died, his friends put his body in a grave. On Easter morning, some women went to the grave. But Jesus' body wasn't inside! God brought him back to life! Jesus was alive again!

*Did Jesus stay in the grave?*
**LUKE 24:1-8**

After Jesus came back to life, he saw two of his old friends. But they didn't know who he was! They still thought Jesus was dead, so they were very sad. But after he spent time with them, they knew he was Jesus. They were so happy that he was alive again!

*When were Jesus' friends happy again?*

**LUKE 24:13-35**

Jesus visited his disciples. They were amazed to see him. He showed them the nail marks in his hands and feet. Jesus stayed on earth for a while. Then one day he rose up in the sky. The disciples watched him go back to heaven. But everyone who loves him will see him someday!

*Where did Jesus go?*
**LUKE 24:36-53**

After Jesus went back to heaven, his friends met together. Suddenly they heard a loud noise like a storm. Then little fires appeared on all their heads. The fire didn't burn them. It was a sign that God's Holy Spirit had come to live in their hearts to help them.

*Who came to live in the hearts of Jesus' friends?*

**ACTS 2:1-4**

The Holy Spirit helped Peter heal a man who had never been able to walk. Peter and John met the man at the temple when they went there to pray. The man asked them for money. But Peter said, "Get up and walk!" Suddenly the man jumped up! He praised God for the miracle.

*Did the Holy Spirit heal the man?*
*Did he need to learn to walk?*
**ACTS 3:1-11**

Stephen loved Jesus. He told people how kind Jesus was. He said that only Jesus could forgive their sins. Some people were very angry with Stephen. They were wicked and threw big rocks at him. Then Stephen died and went to heaven to live with Jesus forever.

*Where did Stephen go when he died?*
**ACTS 6:8-15; 7:51-60**

Philip was God's friend. God sent him to talk to a man riding in a chariot. Philip told the man about God. The man listened. Then he wanted to be God's friend too. Philip said the man could be God's friend if he believed in Jesus. God wants to be everyone's friend.

*Are you God's friend?*
**ACTS 8:26-38**

Paul was Jesus' enemy. He hurt and killed people who loved Jesus. One day Paul saw a bright light that blinded him. He fell down because he couldn't see. Then Jesus talked to him from heaven. Paul decided he wanted to obey Jesus. After that Paul told many other people about Jesus.

*What did Paul do after Jesus talked to him from heaven?*

**ACTS 9:1-28**

Jesus' enemies put Peter in jail. They didn't want Peter to keep telling people that Jesus loves them and died for them. God sent an angel to help Peter. The chains on Peter broke apart so that he could walk. Then the angel opened the jail doors without a key, and Peter walked out!

*How did Peter get out of jail?*
**ACTS 12:1-11**

Timothy's grandmother loved God. She read Bible stories to him. When Timothy grew up, he told lots of people about the Bible and about Jesus. God gave us the Bible. It teaches us about God's love and helps us learn to do what pleases God.

*What does the Bible teach us?*

**2 TIMOTHY 1:3-8; 3:14-17**

Paul was God's enemy for a while. But then he became God's friend. Paul went on a long trip. He sailed on a boat far away from home. He told people in other countries that Jesus died for their sins. He said that Jesus loved them. Paul was a missionary.

*What did Paul tell people in other countries?*

**ACTS 13:4-49**

$P$aul and Silas were in jail because they told everyone about Jesus. But God sent an earthquake that broke open the prison doors. The chains on Paul and Silas flew off! The jailer was afraid they would run away, but they didn't. Paul told him about Jesus. He and his family all believed in Jesus too!

*Who believed in Jesus?*
**ACTS 16:16-34**

Paul's boat sank in a huge storm. Paul and the others swam to land. God kept everyone safe. He had more work for Paul to do as a missionary. God wanted him to tell everyone about Jesus.

*Did God take care of Paul when the boat sank?*

**ACTS 27:1, 13-44**

Paul was in jail again. God let him be there for a long time. God didn't send another earthquake to get Paul out. God still loved him, but he wanted Paul to tell the people in jail about Jesus. God always loves us, even though sometimes he lets us have troubles.

*Did God still love Paul, even when Paul was in jail?*

**ACTS 28:16-31**

J ohn was one of Jesus' best friends when Jesus lived on earth. When John was old, Jesus talked to him in a vision, like a dream. In the vision Jesus told John about things that will happen. Jesus said he is coming back someday! Everyone who believes in him will live with him forever.

*Who will live with Jesus forever?*
**REVELATION 1:1-8; 22:1-7**